Foreword

For many people, depression is still a taboo subject. Out of incomprehension or fear, many prefer to avoid friends, colleagues and neighbours who are ill with depression. So, as though it isn't bad enough to have to deal with the disease, sufferers often also have to live with disbelief, anger or embarrassment from those around them. Or – sometimes almost worse – clumsy attempts to cheer them up or talk them out of their illness.

If you are a Christian and suffer from depression, the situation can be even worse. Well-meaning friends may suggest that *real* Christians don't get depressed, or that you are resisting God's healing power.

So this book is a great debunker of myths. Its author describes, with painful honesty, what her own experience of depression felt like and how it constricted and deformed her life over a long period of time. There is no self-pity in this description. Instead, it is offered as a lifeline. Those who are still in the arid wilderness of depression will be able to recognise their own symptoms and know that they are not the only ones to have felt so completely alone, while those who live with someone who is severely depressed will be helped to understand how to offer companionship and love to someone who cannot yet respond.

Through her illness, Katharine came to a profound reassessment of Jesus, which she is now able to offer to others. At the heart of what she offers is the discovery that, unlike friends and relations, God is not embarrassed, ashamed or frightened of this disease of depression. God longs only for good things for those who suffer and, even when we can see no signs of it at all, God is working to free those who are held captive by the power of depression.

The book dispels fear and keeps hope alive. Because Katharine has herself walked through the wilderness, she knows there is a path that leads out, and she offers herself as guide.

It will be clear to all who read this book, as well as to the many, many people who know Katharine's other work, that her experience has given her depth and insight. God did not want Katharine to suffer from depression, and does not want that for anyone else, either. But neither is God wasteful. In God's skilful hands, even dross can be spun into gold.

Katharine is a regular writer for Redemptorist Publications. As well as contributing to *Common Worship Living Word*, *Sunday Link* and *Live the Word*, Katharine has also written *The Way of the Cross*. She is a Reader in the Church of England. You can find out more about her and her work at www.katharinesmith.org.uk.

It has been a privilege to work with Katharine on this book.

Jane Williams
Editor

I've got to hope that somehow all this mess and misery will be redeemed, but hope's hard sometimes particularly when you're in pain. It's hard when you're enduring Good Friday to imagine the dawning of Easter Day.

Susan Howatch
A Question of Integrity
(London: Little, Brown, 1997)

However mixed our motives in writing (or reading) books, in the end they are about our desire to share (and learn more about) what it means to be human and what matters to us most, our desire "to speak what we feel, not what we ought to say". For those who write such books... they aim to be, in short, a small – and sometimes quite risky – act of love.

Michael Mayne
The Enduring Melody
(London: Darton, Longman & Todd, 2006)

Hello. I don't know who you are or what has brought you to this page but welcome

If you are here because you need hope and encouragement in your journey in the wilderness, then I picture you as someone whose life has been clouded either by your own experience of depression and anxiety or by the experience of someone close to you.

Perhaps you struggle with faith when God seems remote, if not absent altogether, and know the despair that pulls you to the brink of giving up on life itself.

Perhaps you are someone who finds there is not enough understanding in the Church about the sort of mental distress that is actually a clinical illness; someone who longs for a God who really can redeem the sheer hell that is living with depression, with all its ugliness and debilitating symptoms.

I picture you as someone like me and I want to write something that can speak to you from a shared experience, from a shared knowledge that the Good News of Jesus Christ has to reach into that valley of the shadow of death.

I write also from a place that is beyond depression, a place where there is hope and strength, faith and a joy in life that at one time seemed utterly unattainable.

I wish I could say that I got here because I've found a quick and easy fix, that my depression is completely cured, and the illness never bothers me now. It hasn't been like that. What I can say is that in this place I "manage" my illness through medication, adapting my lifestyle and being realistic about my vulnerability to more episodes of depression.

Now that my life, work and relationships are no longer dominated by misery, anxiety and emotional need, I want to look again at the Gospel stories but through a different lens. I want to see what they have to say to those of us walking in the valley of shadow that is depression. I want to find out what they offer to someone held captive by crippling anxiety and panic attacks. If Jesus came that we may have life in all its abundance, to free captives and heal the sick, then he must be able to offer that life, freedom and healing to all who are tormented by mental distress. He must also offer comfort and strength to those who feel helpless when someone they love or care for seems unreachable and like a stranger because of their disturbed mental state. He must be able to reach me and you.

And I believe he can. I believe passionately in a God who can bring healing into the darkest and most painful experience, redeeming it by using that experience for good and offering new life and hope in what was a barren land, a wilderness.

My long journey through depression and anxiety has been difficult. I know from my own experience that this dreadful illness affects every aspect of our lives from sleeping and eating patterns to our ability to function at school or at work and our personal relationships, which are often distorted or broken by our need, our pain and our despair.

When I was first properly diagnosed with clinical depression I was referred to a psychologist for "talking therapy" and prescribed antidepressants. Those initial months were incredibly difficult and my progress seemed painfully slow. I remember asking God, in prayer but none too politely, why it had to take so long: why couldn't I just get better? God's response (and I do believe it was God's response) was in thoughts and images which unfolded in my mind like this:

The vase

I see an object recovered from deep in the ground, caked with the mud of centuries and unrecognisable from its shape. Experts know that under all that mud is an ancient vase, still intact and exquisitely beautiful. Although anxious to free this vase from its prison, they know that they can't just blast it with water to clean the mud off all at once. If they do that there is a risk that the vase will be broken; it's too delicate to take such violent treatment. Instead they have to work slowly and carefully to remove each layer of earth and mud. It's a painstaking task and takes so long to do, but it means that when the vase finally comes into the light of day it will be in one piece, and as clean and beautiful as it was the day it was made.

That was a response I could understand, even though it wasn't quite what I wanted. I've held on to it over the years and it has almost always given me strength and determination not to give up on the healing process.

I invite you to walk with me on this exploration in the search for healing. I hope that our thoughts, ideas and prayers along the way will support you in your journey of healing and growth. They are offered in love as I believe they were offered to me.

Caring for people who suffer from depression

I hope that this book will also be useful to those who care for and support people suffering from depression.

I hope that it will help you to see that the symptoms of the person you love are shared by many, many others. I hope it will also help to strengthen your own faith, and give you some insights into how to be with the person you care for.

It's desperately sad to see someone we love weighed down and choked by depression so that he or she cannot live a normal life. It's hard to see someone with creative gifts or an inspired ministry brought down so low that he or she can barely function or relate to people. It can make us feel furiously angry with the illness and frustrated at our inability to lift the cloud. We might grieve for the loss, albeit temporary, of the person we know and love, and long for his or her return to us safe and well.

If we feel these things for someone we love, we can perhaps get an inkling of how God might feel about it. God loves each of us more than anyone else possibly can. He, too, longs for us to be free and well. He will do everything he can to make his presence known. In the same way he cares for us, the ones who love and grieve, and works for our healing and wholeness as well. We need to be able to trust in that love and rest awhile to recover our own energy and strength.

For those of us who try to support someone we love who is suffering in mind and spirit, it may be our firm belief that healing can and will happen in the life so blighted. At times it will be right to offer an assurance of faith and encouragement. At such times it can help someone to be able to hang on to our faith to steady him or her.

But it's important not to over-emphasise this assurance to someone who is being driven to distraction or despair by negative and painful thoughts and emotions. He or she may be convinced that God is either uninterested, or indifferent, or perhaps even ill-disposed towards him or her. We need to hold on to our own belief in God's loving faithfulness towards us and the person with us, while allowing the other to be true to his or her feelings and experience of anxiety and depression.

This doesn't mean we abandon our friend. We're not saying, "There's nothing we can do but we'll pray for you," and then leaving our friend to go on alone in the dark. Instead, it's about walking beside our friend on the path he or she is travelling. We can't be truly alongside someone if we keep trying to pull that person along our path, or any other path, which for the moment he or she can't take.

Loving someone through this journey is very costly, and carers, too, may find themselves in some scary and risky places. But God, who makes a way in the wilderness and rivers in the desert, still says to us all, "I am with you."

In the first part of the book, I describe my own journey through the wilderness of depression, in the hope that it will give you some comfort to know that others have felt alone and afraid like you and want to reach out to you in love.

In the second part, I offer you some of the "angels" whom I met in the wilderness. In particular, through encounters with Jesus, as he is found in Mark's Gospel, I hope to make it clear that depression is not sinful or in some way your fault, and that here, as in all of human life, Jesus is with us.

Part One

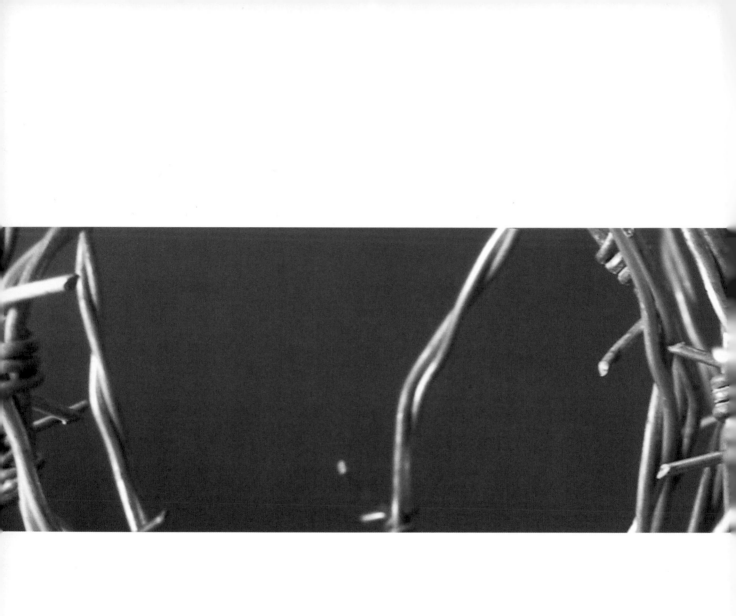

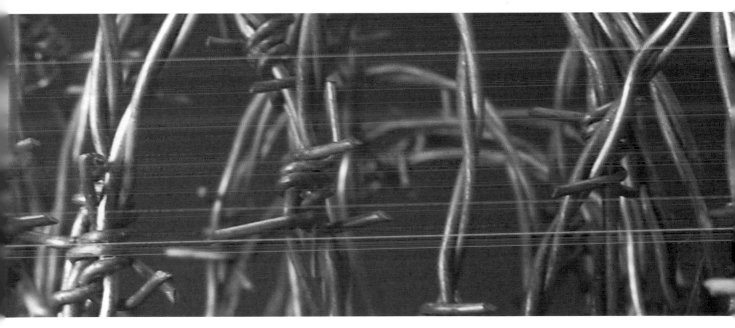

The Wilderness *of* Depression

My own story
What's it like to be depressed?

Perhaps the first thing to do is to identify what we mean by depression and the symptoms that are commonly experienced in varying degrees of severity.

Sometimes when people have had a bad day, the weather's awful and they feel fed up, they say they're depressed. This is not the sort of depression this book is about. Depression is a clinical illness, a medical condition with far-reaching effects on our lives.

Let's have a look at the most common symptoms of this illness. We may not all experience every one of these but we will almost certainly recognise many of them in ourselves or in people we care about.

- *Low mood for most of the day, nearly every day. Things always seem "black".*
- *Loss of enjoyment and interest in life, even for activities that you normally enjoy.*
- *Abnormal sadness, often with weepiness.*
- *Feelings of guilt, worthlessness, or uselessness.*
- *Poor motivation. Even simple tasks seem difficult.*
- *Poor concentration. It may be difficult to read, work, etc.*
- *Sleeping problems:*
    - *» sometimes difficulty in getting off to sleep,*
    - *» sometimes waking early and unable to get back to sleep.*
    - *» Sometimes sleeping too much.*
    - *» Lacking in energy, always tired.*

- *Difficulty with affection, including going off sex.*
- *Poor appetite and weight loss. Sometimes the reverse happens with comfort eating and weight gain.*
- *Irritability, agitation or restlessness.*
- *Symptoms often seem worse first thing each day.*
- *Physical symptoms such as headaches, palpitations, chest pains and general aches.*
- *Recurrent thoughts of death. This is not usually a fear of death, more a preoccupation with death and dying. Some people get suicidal ideas such as "life's not worth living".*

Whatever our symptoms are, we may also recognise that the whole experience of depression is greater than the sum of its parts. Overshadowing all that we can put into words, it probably feels like there is an intangible "something" beyond words which weighs us down and seems to separate us from our true selves and from others, leaving us feeling isolated and alone.

In this very real experience of depression, loneliness and isolation we may lose sight of other realities, and I've found these words of St Paul helpful when I'm struggling with my faith and feeling isolated from God:

> *I am convinced that there is nothing in death or life,*
> *in the realm of spirits or superhuman powers,*
> *in the world as it is or the world as it shall be,*
> *in the forces of the universe, in heights or depths –*
> *nothing in all creation that can separate us*
> *from the love of God in Christ Jesus our Lord.*

Romans 8:38-39

How did we get here?

The ways in which we arrived in this wilderness are as individual as the many ways in which we experience depression. For some, it's a gradual slide down into the pit, while for others it may seem to come out of the blue with a force that knocks us off our feet and into a sort of waking nightmare.

How can this happen? I'd like to offer some thoughts about this experience which may be familiar to others.

Physical pain alerts our brain to the fact that some harm is being done to our bodies. It might be a relatively minor injury or it could be a symptom of something which needs urgent attention. We ourselves make judgements about how we should react to pain, depending on its cause and, if need be, we consult a doctor, a dentist or other medical advisor.

In a similar way, depression can be the way our minds warn us that something in our lives is harming us and needs attention. Perhaps we're not so good at picking up on these symptoms and acting to relieve the distress and strain we feel.

Depression, anxiety and stress are very closely connected. We know that a certain amount of stress is good for us and, at the right level, is healthy. The problem arises when our stress levels are very high over long periods of time and rarely, if ever, come down to a normal pitch.

We can start to feel like a performer on stage trying to spin plates. He dashes around trying to restart a plate's spin before it smashes on the floor, but as fast as he does that other plates need attention, and more plates appear to increase the tension yet further. He daren't stop for a second in case they all end up smashed.

So we carry on spinning all the commitments and responsibilities in our lives and daren't stop, because how would the world go on turning without us?

Or perhaps our stress has a focus within our emotional and mental life – unseen but incredibly powerful and debilitating: old traumas, memories, present fears and confusions, grief, anger, self-hatred. All these things take their toll on our ability to live

healthy, balanced lives. The effect can be like trying to drive a car with both accelerator and brakes full on. We're driven forward and away from our centre by these emotional forces but also frozen into indecision and inactivity, drained of energy and motivation. In the end it may well be that the car takes the decision out of the driver's hands by juddering to a full stop.

We all experience the "final straw" in different ways and over different periods of time but at some point we realise that things have got out of control and we need help.

> *That morning seemed to be like any other morning. I was stressed and overloaded at work; I didn't really want to be in that job but couldn't find another; I felt trapped financially and frustrated by the apparent lack of opportunity to be creative in my life. I was struggling with some very deeply ingrained emotional issues and suffering sleeplessness and migraines. But I was coping, making the best of things, taking new responsibilities in an attempt to make my job more satisfying. But that morning, for some reason, my whole mental and emotional system shut down. I just started crying and couldn't stop. I stayed at home that day and it was a year before I worked again.*

I'd been ill with depression most of my life but this was a turning point. It was the moment when I was aware that something in me had to change radically and permanently. My old ways of coping were no longer working. I needed to find new ways of being and new ways of relating to the world and people around me.

There is no doubt in my mind that living through the experience of depression changes us at a very deep level and sometimes in unexpected ways.

In this experience of coming apart and brokenness we are undergoing a form of rebirth. It's not an experience anyone would choose to go through and I still have many questions about why it has to be so painful and prolonged. All I can say is that there can come a point where we look back at the darkness and despair and forward to the light and hope of new life, and know that it was worth the struggle.

"Listen! A sower went out to sow... Some [seed] fell among thistles; and the thistles grew up and choked the corn, and it produced no crop."

He went on: "Do you not understand this parable? How then are you to understand any parable?"

"With others again the seed falls among thistles; they hear the word, but worldly cares and the false glamour of wealth and evil desires of all kinds come in and choke the word, and it proves barren."

Mark 4:3, 7, 13, 18-19

Clearing the thistles — the cost of recovery

It may seem strange to use the parable of the sower to illustrate an aspect of depression and recovery but for me it offers a powerful picture of some of the things that can cause the illness and what it may cost us to travel along the road to recovery.

I've always felt a bit sorry for the soil that had thistles growing on it. If thistles were growing it must have been reasonably good soil, with sufficient nutrients to support life and growth. It must have had a good balance of sun and rain, and if only those thistles had been cleared the soil might have produced an excellent crop.

If only... if only... Probably we could all spend a lot of time thinking how different our lives would have been if only this hadn't happened or that had. Few of us, I imagine, get through life without regrets, without wishing we could put the clock back to some defining moment and change it.

Regrets and yearnings like that can in themselves be a trigger for depression. The burden of guilt, the weight of sadness and the grief that comes with a sense of loss can all be too much to bear, and depression throws a suffocating, choking cloud over those emotions, flattening them so they can't hurt us so much.

Perhaps we've been carrying those suppressed emotions around with us for an awfully long time, maybe even from birth or very early childhood. We may not remember what started it, we may not even realise anything's wrong until, for whatever reason, the emotions begin breaking out and creating havoc in our minds.

Once depression has got a hold on us and controls our emotions it can be very painful and threatening when we start feeling again. When our foot "goes to sleep" and is numb, the process of getting blood flowing to restore normality is quite painful. We call it "pins and needles" because of the sensation of lots of small stabbing pains.

So it is with recovery from depression. The process is painful but necessary. Clearing thistles from the soil of our being does hurt but it's the only way, if we are to realise our potential and wholeness.

"If only…" can be overwhelming. We might catch a glimpse of light and hope ahead, but that light shows us even more clearly the things we regret, the time spent paralysed by this illness and how far we still have to go.

The temptation to give up can be very strong at this point and at least the darkness is familiar. We know how to live in its suffocating gloom. We can't be disappointed, either, because there's no risk in taking that path.

The alternative is to believe in that glimpse of light and hope; to believe that one day the glimpse will become a clear vision and surround us with healing and peace. Moving forward seems daunting, it's not an easy option; but somewhere deep within us God is always working to bring us to wholeness and joy, and he promises to be with us. He doesn't wait at the other end of the tunnel until we pull ourselves through. He walks alongside us in the tunnel and travels along the path, clearing thistles from around our souls as we walk.

Take up your cross and the truth shall set you free

I'd like to take a moment now to think about how depression can affect the way we interpret things. For example, because our emotions are flattened and our mood is low we can't enjoy the things we used to: radio or television comedies won't make us laugh, thrillers won't be exciting, music won't be relaxing, and difficult problems that once we might have coped with can assume huge proportions and seem insurmountable.

Being depressed can also make us totally self-centred in the way we perceive things: everything relates to us and our condition. Or the opposite can be true – we are totally out of touch with everyday life.

The following passage is an example of one of the sayings of Jesus that I have often struggled with and find very difficult to read or hear without applying it to my own state of mind when I'm depressed.

Then Jesus called the people to him, as well as his disciples,
and said to them, "Anyone who wants to be a follower of
mine must renounce self; he must take up his cross and
follow me. Whoever wants to save his life will lose it, but
whoever loses his life for my sake and for the Gospel's will
save it. What does anyone gain by winning the whole world
at the cost of his life? What can he give to buy his life back?"

Mark 8:34-37

I'm not sure that anyone finds this passage easy to understand. What does it mean to take up your cross (a hideous instrument of torture and death) and to lose your life for the sake of Jesus and the Gospel? How on earth does this fit in with Jesus saying he came that we may have life in all its abundance?For me depression, with its negative and destructive characteristics, casts a very dark shadow over these words. We may find during the healing process that some sort of denial or quashing of ourselves is behind at least part of our problems with depression. For example:

• *Perhaps we learned very early on in life that it wasn't safe to be angry, sad or afraid. Such emotions were frowned upon and brought disapproval and reproof.*

• *Perhaps our gifts and talents were never recognised or encouraged and so we never developed them.*

• *Perhaps we were never considered to be worth attention or love and we grew up with such a low opinion of ourselves that we never attend to our own needs or consider ourselves to be in any way equal to others.*

The chances are that if we have had to deny ourselves in this sense we also carry an awful lot of anger. If we then have to keep that anger suppressed as well, it's no wonder if eventually we erupt like a volcano and spew out all the negative stuff that's been building up under the surface.

Depression very often carries with it a huge amount of suppressed anger and it can be very frightening for everyone when that anger starts finding outlets for its expression. If this is the case then part of any therapeutic intervention must be to find safe ways for anger to be experienced and released safely for all concerned.

If in this process of releasing suppressed feelings and aspects of our personalities we're suddenly faced with the demand that we renounce (or deny) ourselves and carry our cross, we might well feel as if we've hit a brick wall. What happened to the compassion, love and wish for our healing? Is that now withdrawn, leaving us to face yet more hurt and misery?

Everything that's healthy in me protests that that interpretation can't be right. It just doesn't fit with the image of Jesus that's been forming in my mind over the years of recovery.

I've reached a place now where I can read commentaries about this passage and gain some intellectual insights into what Jesus is saying and what it might mean to us when we follow him. However, I haven't

yet got past my earlier emotional reaction. Instead, I've found a way of honouring my perception of these words and making sense of them that is in keeping with my image of Jesus and his way of truth.

I fully accept that what follows may bear no relation at all to what Jesus is "really" talking about here. However, it comes from a lot of struggling and thinking and might make sense in the context of this book, even though it wouldn't belong in any scholarly or academic essay on the subject!

When we follow Jesus we are following the one who is "the Way" and "the Truth" and we, too, are called to be true and honest. The truth will show us realities about ourselves and our lives that may

well be painful to acknowledge, but which we need to see and understand before we are free to be the people God wants us to be.

I think that, whether or not we suffer from depression, we're all aware that we fall far short of our own ideals, never mind God's perfection, and at some time we all experience a sense of regret and sadness and the wish to change for the better.

So let's set out on this part of our pilgrimage with a willingness to be truthful about ourselves and to receive God's truth, which really can set us free.

Our first step is to think about what our "cross" is. What is it that we have to pick up and carry in order to follow Jesus?

Men who were to be crucified would be made to carry the cross-beam, to which their arms were to be nailed, to the place of crucifixion where it would be fixed to an upright to form the shape of a cross.

So to carry our cross means to carry an instrument of our own torture and death. It represents shame, guilt and an agony that will torment body and mind. There is no hiding from the meaning of this cross, no running away from its reality or avoiding our inevitable fate.

Is it overstating the case to say that being ill with depression brings upon us something of these experiences?

Psychological torment and mental pain are impossible to measure and invisible to the human eye, but they are real and frightening. Feelings of shame and guilt are also often present and we cannot run away from ourselves or avoid our distorted thoughts and emotions.

The next stage is to consider what it means to "take up" this cross, this darkness we call depression.

Perhaps it's about acknowledging and accepting that we are ill and need some sort of specialist treatment. Facing up to this reality can be very scary. It means perhaps feeling powerless against a disease that can't be put right quickly and easily, feeling that we have lost control of our lives and facing a lot of uncertainty about the future.

We may carry in our minds the idea that "Christians don't or shouldn't

get depressed", which is manifestly not true, but has often been said by people who may not realise how cruel and damaging their words can be.

For some of us, though, realising that what we're experiencing is an illness which involves imbalances of certain chemicals and hormones can come as a huge relief. If we've been battling with debilitating symptoms and struggling to cope with everyday life, not understanding why we can no longer do so, it can make all the difference to hear a doctor tell us that we have a recognised illness and there is medication to help. In that sense the truth does set us free to begin dealing with the illness itself.

"What does anyone gain by winning the whole world at the cost of his or her mental health, sense of well-being and personal fulfilment? What can he or she give to buy those things back?"

Quite often, I think, going through a prolonged period of depression can lead us to reflect on what's really important in our lives. We are not likely to wish to repeat the experience and indeed will look for ways to prevent this happening. Some of us may have to examine our lives very carefully, being prepared to do whatever's necessary to bring about a change in our circumstances or ways of being which will improve our state of mind.

In this sense we may have to be prepared to "lose" at least part of our lives as we know them. We may have to accept that we need to "lose" certain attitudes and ways of relating to people if we are to enjoy more healthy and meaningful relationships and lifestyles.

As we work to "lose" what is unhealthy in our lives we are also searching for the good, the wholesome and fulfilling life which God has always wanted for us. This God-given life is our true life that can be saved when we make it our treasure, worth everything we have and all of who we are.

It may appear that looking at this passage in the way we have in this part of the book is very self-centred, very self-absorbed and therefore contrary to its "real" meaning about selfless love and suffering for the sake of the Gospel.

That may well be so, but it's also true that until our "selves" are healthy and strong and free from the constant pain of mental distress we are unlikely to be able to give of ourselves or to love as God loves us. For a while, at least, we will need to make our own health a priority, and I believe God knows that and understands with compassion: "he will not break a crushed reed or snuff out a smouldering wick"

(Isaiah 42:3).

The valley of the shadow of death

When I was very ill with depression and unable to work (or do anything much), I did try to go to Morning Prayer daily. It gave me a reason to get up and dressed for nine o'clock and the fellowship and prayer with three or four others who regularly attended were important to me.

Sometimes it was extremely difficult to cope. There is an opening section in the Anglican Morning Prayer service in *Common Worship* which says:

> *The night has passed*
> *and the day lies open before us.*
> *Let us pray with one heart and mind.*
> *As we rejoice in the gift of this new day,*
> *so may the light of your presence, O God,*
> *set our hearts on fire with love for you;*
> *now and for ever. Amen.*

These words are such an antithesis of what was going on in my heart and mind that they actually provide a useful framework for me to describe what, in my experience, it is like to be walking in the valley of shadow that is called depression.

"the night has passed..."

It was a long, restless night. I went to sleep quite quickly because I have pills to help with that. I had very vivid and disturbing dreams in which I was experiencing deep emotions of grief or fear. These feelings have stayed with me since I woke up and will take hours to fade away. I woke up early, much too early, with a sickening sense of disappointment that I had done so. I lay awake with my mind in turmoil, wishing I could go back to sleep and worrying about what is happening to me.

"and the day lies open before us..."

A long, long day lies ahead filled with an empty nothingness. I dread the hours to come, with no hope of improvement. I have no sense of purpose, and I'm beyond wanting to do anything, whilst also not wanting to do nothing. Everything seems pointless, so why bother anyway?

"as we rejoice in the gift of this new day…"

It's not a gift, it's more like a curse, and I feel so guilty for thinking that. I have no rejoicing in me and I don't want to face a "new" day which I know will be like all the others have been over the last weeks and months. I want the day to be over so I can go back to sleep, or I'll take some pills so I sleep during the day. There is no promise or hope, freshness or sense of a new beginning, there is just this overwhelming dreadful darkness leading me relentlessly towards total despair.

"so may the light of your presence, O God…"

God has forsaken me, left me alone, abandoned me because I am so wretched and worthless. It's pointless to pray like this; how can the light of God's presence reach me here anyway? This is the valley of the shadow of death, and I am very afraid.

"set our hearts on fire with love for you…"

My heart is deadened, with not a spark of fire or love. The only emotions I am able to feel are the destructive ones of fear, anger, hatred and despair. I don't believe there is a way in which I can be "fired up" into hope and love. It's just too much to cope with when I know I'll have to go through this awful sequence of thoughts and feelings tomorrow morning, the morning after that and who knows how many more mornings after that? I'm so tired, I just want it all to end.

We saw earlier that a preoccupation with death and suicidal thoughts are symptoms of depression. I think it's quite probable that most people who suffer from the illness do, at some point, think about suicide.

- *We may not think about it as a real possibility for us but we may find ourselves thinking "what if...?"*

- *These thoughts may occur to us too often to ignore; we may fear for ourselves that suicide is a way out we'll take one day.*

- *We may have reached the point where we are seriously considering it and even beginning to make plans.*

- *We may fear that even thinking about suicide is sinful. Therefore we cannot risk talking to other Christians who may condemn and reject us.*

I want to say first of all that, in my opinion, despair and suicidal thoughts are not in themselves sinful. They are, I'm afraid, part of being human and need to be accepted as such, so that we can talk openly about them and seek ways in which we can grow through them towards embracing life once more.

In my personal experience, suicidal thoughts have been in my mind in two sets of circumstances:

- *as an extreme emotional response to an event or situation which I had found unbearable and from which I just wanted a quick exit;*

or

- *as a very calm and logical way to respond to my situation when I just couldn't see any way through.*

Some people talk about suicide as "doing something silly". Others say that taking your own life is very selfish because it causes so much anguish to relatives and friends left behind. I'm very aware of the need for sensitivity here because I don't want in any way to deny or minimise the grief, pain and possibly anger of anyone bereaved by suicide. However, I can understand, I think, the sort of train of thought that might lead to people taking their own lives, believing it to be the best way out for themselves and for those who love them. It might go something like this:

- *I am desperately unhappy, ill and despairing.*
- *I can't imagine ever recovering from this; I've lost all hope of feeling better.*
- *I know my family and friends love me and want me to be well, and I can see how my illness affects them.*
- *But I cannot get well either for my own sake or for theirs.*
- *It would be better for all of us if I ended this pain so they can move on.*

If you yourself have suicidal thoughts or you are supporting someone who may be feeling this way, it is important that you get help and support immediately. As a first stop you might find it helpful to contact the Samaritans.

www.samaritans.org; email jo@samaritans.org; tel. 08457 909090 [within UK]; address Chris, PO Box 9090, Stirling, United Kingdom FK8 2SA.

They offer twenty-four-hour support to people who are depressed and to carers. Whatever time you ring, day or night, there will be someone on the end of a phone who understands and isn't afraid of such self-destructive thoughts, and who will stay with you for as long as you want them to.

The Samaritans' website is full of information and guidance, including for carers who may themselves be feeling isolated with their own levels of hope being rapidly depleted.

We are probably at our most isolated and lonely when we're in the deep darkness of the valley of the shadow of death. If that's where you are at the moment, I am so sorry that you are suffering in this way. You may not believe me but, please, somehow hang on to a thread of hope that you will get through and life will be worth living again.

If you can find no hope at all, please try to lean on the hope and prayers of others to get you through. One day you will look back and be glad that you chose life, which will seem more precious than it ever did before.

Part Two

Mark 12:41–44

Looking *to* Jesus *for* Help

Images of Jesus

During our time in the wilderness of depression we may find ourselves facing challenges about our own images of Jesus and our relationship with him. These challenges and the resulting struggle may go to the very heart of what we believe about ourselves and how we relate to other people and to God.

I'd like to spend some time reflecting on what image of Jesus we carry in our minds: whether it's a healthy and positive image or one that's got a little distorted and unhelpful, and so might hold us back from fully engaging with the Gospel stories.

Let's look at some relatively straightforward examples:

- *An image of Jesus as the baby lying in a manger may hide from us Jesus the man, fully human and experiencing all that that means – loving, grieving, celebrating, suffering and dying.*

- *An image of Jesus as "gentle Jesus, meek and mild" may prevent us from seeing the angry, impatient Jesus who is outraged by injustices and has no time for hypocrisy and self-righteousness.*

- *There's even a risk that images of the crucified Jesus will keep us fixed on the suffering and pain of being human and prevent us from living in the great promise and hope of the resurrection life that lies beyond.*

These images are true, but none of them on their own gives a complete picture of what Jesus was like when he lived among us.

We may also be carrying within us images that are distorted because of our own personal experiences or relationships. Let's look at these examples:

- *Someone who has grown up among humourless and disapproving adults may well have difficulty in seeing Jesus enjoying himself and accepting all who come to him.*

- *Strict and punishing adults may create a similar image of Jesus in the minds of children who, as they grow older, aren't able to recognise in Jesus a willingness to forgive and to be gentle. They always expect his judgement and a penalty.*

- *A child living with neglectful and often absent adults in a chaotic environment may in later life be unable to believe that Jesus can be trusted.*

The examples could go on. The point is that recognising, acknowledging, understanding and then dismantling these distorted images is an important part of our journey towards healing and wholeness. However, in going through this process, we may need to "work" on our past experiences, and the effect they have had on our cognitive and emotional development, and for that we may well need good professional support and guidance. It may be that our minds had very good reasons for hiding certain things from our consciousness, and we need to respect that and be cautious about the uncovering process which may be incredibly painful. Our general state may get worse before it can get better.

So there's risk involved in the healing process, but the God who calls us to wholeness will also protect us along the way.

The following is an extract from a sermon I preached a couple of years after a severe and prolonged period of depression. It was a terrible time but it was also a turning point in my life and I drew on something of that experience for my sermon.

I began by talking in general terms about images of Jesus that may be unhelpful or which prevent us from seeing what Jesus is really like.

I then went on to say:

Sometimes we don't even realise what our images of Jesus are until they're challenged by our experience in life.

Recently I realised that I had got stuck with an inadequate image of Jesus which was getting in the way. Many people came to Jesus for healing because they were said to be possessed by demons. It's generally accepted now that they were probably suffering from mental disorders which were not identified as such two thousand years ago.

Jesus' response was always to cast the demons out and free the sufferer from his or her affliction then and there.

My image of Jesus from these stories led me to think that I should be able to ask Jesus to cure me of my mental distress and he would do it instantly, like casting out a demon. Because that didn't happen I was angry with him.

I needed to see beyond that image of Jesus casting out demons.

Only then could I encounter the Jesus who had always been walking with me and who would continue to walk with me, my doctors and my friends through the painful, slow journey towards healing. It was only then that I could encounter the Jesus who knows me better than I know myself, who wants my healing as much as I do and who knows how best that can happen.

That experience has taught me that whatever images of Jesus we carry, if they prevent us encountering the risen Christ who can lead us into new life then it's worth taking the risk of questioning them and being open to seeing Jesus in new ways.

Two new images of Jesus

I'd like now to offer two images of Jesus which speak to me of his love, compassion and understanding. They are images that have come into my mind during periods of illness and I hope they might also speak to you.

The first is of Jesus leaving Jericho and meeting blind Bartimaeus (Mark 10:46-52). Bartimaeus has been shouting and shouting at Jesus, "Son of David, Jesus, have pity on me!" Although others try to silence him, Jesus stops and calls Bartimaeus to him.

Now we might think that, since Bartimaeus is blind, it's perfectly obvious what he wants from Jesus. Surely he must want his sight restored?

Jesus, though, takes nothing for granted. He asks the question:

What do you want me to do for you?

I was reading this story one day when these words seemed to jump off the page at me. I felt almost as if Jesus was asking me that question. I had a vivid picture in my mind of Jesus, the servant king, kneeling before me and asking, "What do you want me to do for you?"

It was an extraordinary experience and it made me think about how I would answer.

Perhaps it's a question Jesus asks each of us at some point, inviting us to think about our answer, taking nothing for granted.

When we're depressed it might seem perfectly obvious that we would want to be lifted up out of that pit and into daylight again. Indeed that may be our immediate response:

I want you to set me free from this illness.

Although the healing may not be immediately obvious, I believe this moment will be a marker along the road to recovery, a time when some significant change and growth is possible.

There may be times, though, when our answer to Jesus is more about getting through another day, coping with one more doctor's appointment, making one necessary phone call.

Whenever we feel that we just can't do anything for ourselves, perhaps we could try to bring to mind this image of Jesus, the servant king, calling us to him as he called Bartimaeus, and asking us the question:

The second image I'd like to offer is that of Jesus sitting opposite the temple treasury, watching people dropping money into the chest:

> *Many rich people were putting in large amounts. Presently there came a poor widow who dropped in two tiny coins, together worth a penny. He called his disciples to him and said, "Truly I tell you: this poor widow has given more than all those giving to the treasury; for the others who have given had more than enough, but she, with less than enough, has given all that she had to live on."*
>
> Mark 12:41-44

I wonder if the widow of this story ever knew that someone had noticed her plight and understood how much it cost her to give a very small amount of money. I hope so, especially if she felt embarrassed or ashamed of being unable to give more.

I draw hope and comfort from this story when I'm unable to cope with the activities, conversations and workloads that others seem to take in their stride.

We may all find many things more difficult and tiring when we're ill, and if we have a physical ailment, people understand that. If we're recovering from a broken leg or a heart problem, it's OK to be exhausted after a fairly short walk or to want to stay at home resting rather than go out for an evening with friends. It may not be so easy for people to understand extreme tiredness, unwillingness to socialise or inability to concentrate at work when we seem on the outside to be well.

This picture of Jesus at the temple treasury tells me that he understands what's going on beneath the surface. He knows how much it costs us some days just to get out of bed and dressed. He knows the effort it takes to tackle any task and the distress that very minor problems can cause.

Jesus won't criticise or put pressure on us when we just can't cope with life as we would if we were well. He will, though, appreciate, respect and value what we do achieve even if by the standards of others it looks very little.

For me these are powerful images of Jesus as the compassionate servant king who understands how depression affects our lives and who reaches out to offer us help.

And when we feel frustrated, guilty or inadequate because of our lack of energy, enthusiasm or ability to function as we used to, we can perhaps think of the widow giving all that she could afford, perhaps even more, and remember that Jesus may be more forgiving, understanding and compassionate towards us than we sometimes are to ourselves.

We may believe that we have little in common with the people Jesus encountered during his ministry on earth. After all, they lived two thousand years ago in an entirely different culture and without our knowledge and understanding of nature, science and medicine. Yet if we look more closely we will come to recognise ourselves and our experiences in their stories. Their encounters with Jesus, which have so much to tell us about how he would be towards us, can offer us encouragement as we struggle with our own difficulties and diseases.

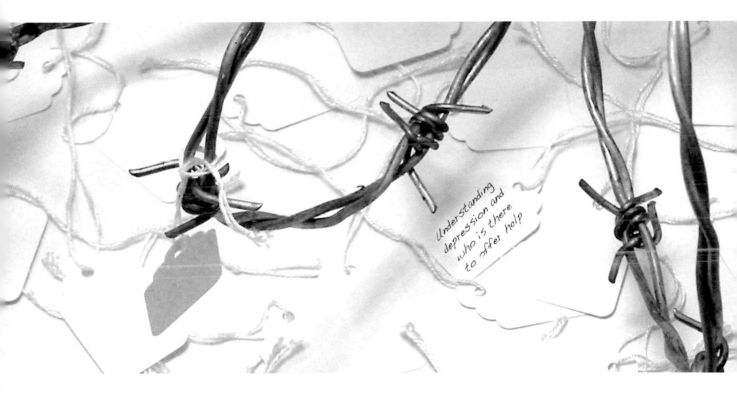

Understanding
depression and
who is there
to offer help

Healing encounters with Jesus in Mark's Gospel
Beginning our journey through the wilderness

We've probably all heard the story of a couple who get lost as they drive around unfamiliar countryside looking for a certain village. They stop to ask directions. And the gentleman they ask stands for a moment scratching his head and then says, "Well, if you're going there I wouldn't start from here."

I know what he means. Sometimes you need to get somewhere else before you can really set off in the right direction.

But when we're stuck here in the wilderness, weighed down with depression and without much hope of getting out of it any time soon, we need someone to point us in the right direction, to offer us hope and assure us that we can get to there from here.

We need good news in our wilderness:

The beginning of the Gospel of Jesus Christ the Son of God. In the prophet Isaiah it stands written:

I am sending my herald ahead of you;
he will prepare your way.
A voice cries in the wilderness,
"Prepare the way for the Lord;
clear a straight path for him."

John the Baptist appeared in the wilderness proclaiming a baptism in token of repentance, for the forgiveness of sins.

Mark 1:1-4

John is the herald of good news and his work as herald is done in the wilderness, right where we are, right now. "Prepare the way for the Lord, clear a straight path for him," because he's coming out here to find us, to bring us out of the wilderness with him.

The wilderness is a desert. It's a barren place where wild animals roam and very little vegetation can grow. There's not much water either, so it's very inhospitable.

When we're depressed it can seem that life has dried up. Just surviving is a huge effort and we lose whatever imagination and creativity we once had. Well, we don't lose it, we just can't reach it at the moment, and we're too exhausted and downhearted to try.

The wilderness is a place of change and transition. It was the place where the people of Israel travelled from slavery in Egypt to freedom in the promised land. They came under attack, suffered from lack of food and water, and even looked back fondly at the time when they were oppressed and exploited.

But it was also the place where God protected them, gave them manna, his food, to eat and brought water out of rocks. It was a place of close communion with God, a time of discovering who they were as a people and how they were to live when they did have their own land.

For us, too, this wilderness in time, this desert of depression and misery, can be a place of change and transition. We will suffer hardship and sometimes wonder if it's worth the struggle, but it will be: that is God's promise. We can come out of this with a new vision for our life and how we want to live it. It probably doesn't seem like it, but we will be closer to God and when we look back we will see that he was here with us right from the start, in the desert.

God was there with Jesus, right from the start, in the desert.

It was at this time that Jesus came from Nazareth in Galilee and was baptised in the Jordan by John. As he was coming up out of the water, he saw the heavens break open and the Spirit descend on him, like a dove. And a voice came from heaven: "You are my beloved Son; in you I take delight."

Mark 1:9-12

As we begin this journey in Mark's Gospel together, it's good to remember this starting point for Jesus, his commitment to God, symbolised by his baptism and God's commitment to him spoken with the words: "You are my beloved Son; in you I take delight."

We also know that Jesus is about to enter into his own wilderness time of temptation as he prepares for his ministry. He will wrestle with thoughts of how he is to carry out that ministry and be tested to the limit in the process.

It's hard to answer the questions, "why does it have to be like this?", "how am I going to get through it?", "Lord, why have you forsaken me?" God doesn't seem to answer those questions. When Moses asked, "Who am I that I should approach Pharaoh and that I should bring the Israelites out of Egypt?" God answered Moses: "I am with you." His answer to us is the same: "I am with you."

Please try to hang on to that promise even when it doesn't feel true, *especially* when it doesn't feel true. One day we will *know* it's true.

For now, today, let us be assured by God that there is a way out of the wilderness; we can get through and out the other side and, most importantly, each of us is a child of God in whom he takes delight. God is not waiting for us to be better or to feel any different before joining us. He is alongside us here and now, *just as we are.*

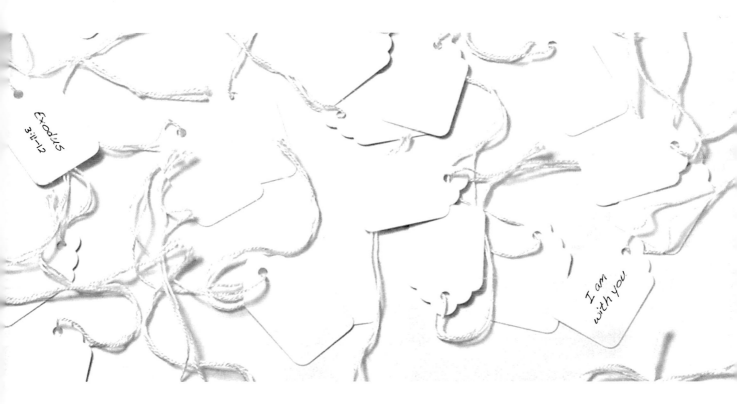

Exodus
3:11–12

I am
with you

We are loved just as we are

When Jesus was having a meal in Levi's house, many tax-collectors and sinners were seated with him and his disciples, for there were many of them among his followers. Some scribes who were Pharisees, observing the company in which he was eating, said to his disciples, "Why does he eat with tax-collectors and sinners?"

Hearing this, Jesus said to them, "It is not the healthy who need a doctor, but the sick; I did not come to call the virtuous, but sinners."

Mark 2:15-17

It sounds so obvious, doesn't it? We only need a doctor if we're ill – ill enough not to be able to treat ourselves with over-the-counter medication.

So why is it that we have such difficulty in believing that we can approach God "just as we are"? Why do we feel we have to be polite and on our best behaviour when we're praying or joining in worship? How can we counter the voice within us that says, "God can see what you're really like, and so can't possibly love you or want you around"?

Does God really only want happy, lively and enthusiastic people around him? Do we really have to be virtuous and loving to be welcomed?

I see myself in a crowd listening to Jesus, following him for miles to hear his words and see miraculous signs. And even though my heart is calling out to him it would never occur to me to approach him myself – I couldn't possibly matter to him. It's enough for me just to be one in the crowd.

He's looking for someone, his eyes search the faces, so many faces, and his close friends also join in the search which gets more and more urgent. Then someone is beside me calling out to Jesus, "She's here, she's here."

Relief on his face, "At last," he says as I am brought to him, "I heard the call of your heart," he says, "but I couldn't find you. Now you are found and all will be well."

Of course not, proclaim the Gospels, which are full of encounters between Jesus and broken, despised, rejected and vulnerable people. What's more he actively seeks them out. He comes to "call" people to him, to find those who are lost or hiding in their shame.

Jesus wants us to be near him, not in spite of our illness but because of it. He wants to heal us and lead us into new life because he knows we can't get there by ourselves.

Let's dare to take him at his word and come to him as sinners and sufferers to receive the forgiveness and healing which he longs to give us.

Before we leave this scene, let's look at how Jesus is with the tax collectors and sinners, and compare it with how others may react to those of us who struggle with mental distress and illness.

Jesus eats a meal with them. He gets alongside those who are despised and excluded from respectable society, and offers them acceptance and friendship. He puts himself outside the social and religious customs of his time, and by doing so attracts disapproval and outrage.

There are people in our own society who regard those with mental illness with fear and suspicion. They avoid the company of such people because they don't know what to expect or how to respond in conversation. In some churches there can also be a sense of disapproval or judgement around a Christian being depressed. If you profess a faith in the Good News of God's kingdom, how can you feel so low and think that life may not be worth living? Needless to say, those sorts of attitudes are incredibly painful for sufferers and add one more layer of misery to the suffocating weights they already carry.

True rock-like friendship is what we need in the valley of shadows. We need friends who can be with us as equals, making no judgements but allowing us to be ourselves. Jesus would sit down and eat a meal with us. He would make us feel that we belong in the world around us. Our conversations with him can be about anything, not just our illness and pain, because he knows and understands what's going on beneath the surface – we don't have to explain it all to him. He isn't afraid of us or our illness, nor is he afraid for himself that he too might become this sick and distressed.

If you care about someone who is depressed but feel there's nothing you can do to help, never underestimate the power of just being there alongside him or her. Rocks don't do much, but they're the best things to hang on to when you feel you're being swept away by some force much stronger than you.

" I am and will be healed"

On one occasion Jesus was approached by a leper, who knelt before him and begged for help.

"If only you will," said that man, "you can make me clean."

Mark 1:40

God longs for us to be well

"If you wanted to heal me, set me free from this dreadful darkness, surely you could do so? The fact that I'm still struggling after all this time with no light ahead must mean that you don't want me to be well."

In the valley of shadows this is a perfectly logical and realistic thing to say to God. How can a God of love allow my spirit, my very self, to be so twisted and racked with unseen pain and distress unless he actually doesn't love me? Indeed he seems to be punishing me for doing something I didn't know I was doing or for being someone I didn't choose to be.

Leprosy has separated this man from his family, his friends and his whole community. So, too, depression and anxiety can cause us to stand outside and away from those whose company we would normally seek out and enjoy.

The effects of mental distress reach beyond the sufferer. When despair or total indifference fills our hearts, those around us, especially those who love us, are likely to sense what's happening and may be afraid of being drawn into the darkness as well. Depression has the ability to feed off the energy and being of another person and so others might avoid us or put up barriers for fear of "contagion".

Others won't talk about our illness or just cannot understand why we are unable to "pull ourselves together" or "snap out of it".

So in some ways we can relate to this leper (a man who is identified by his disease) as we approach Jesus and kneel before him to beg for help. We can beg and plead, our voices can express desperation and also perhaps some anger. Surely there could be anger in those words: "if only you want to, you can make me well".

"You can rescue me from this nightmare and help me to get my life back – **IF** you will."

Jesus was moved to anger.

"Of course I want to heal you. How could you think otherwise? Of course I don't want to see you, or anyone else, suffering disease and distress. Of course I want you to be made whole and to be restored in spirit. I hate all those things that cause pain and misery and I have come to challenge their hold on you, to set you free and help you find fullness of life."

He stretched out his hand [and] touched him.

"I can be with you in the loneliest of places where others cannot reach you. And no matter how much you despise yourself and however isolated you feel, you can never be out of my reach, and to me you can never be untouchable."

The leprosy left him immediately, and he was clean.

We come back to the agonising question about why it takes so long. Why can't our healing be immediately complete?

I wonder if it would help us if we could somehow believe that since God has pronounced us healed and "clean", it's as if we already are. In one sense the healing has taken place, "for the mouth of the Lord has spoken it" and there is no other outcome possible. At the same time, though, the healing must reveal itself in us at the pace we can bear. God isn't really interested in emergency first aid – his healing love is about rebuilding and "doing a new thing" in our lives. And that takes time and energy, just as it took time, energy and extreme care to free my vase from all its mud. But if somehow a mustard seed of hope that says, "I am and will be healed" can germinate within us, we will already be setting off on the right path.

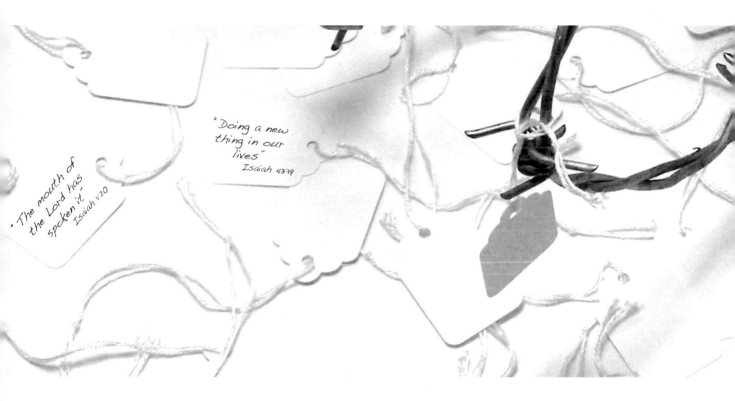

"Doing a new thing in our lives"
Isaiah 43:19

"The mouth of the Lord has spoken it."
Isaiah 1:20

The paralysis of depression

It's quite hard to describe the paralysis of depression. It feels like the loss of the power of thinking and decision-making which prevents the mind from coping with everyday life, never mind problem-solving and abstract, creative thought. It's a form of mental exhaustion too, a state of being where the mind really does seem to have power over the body and uses that power to make any sort of physical exertion quite impossible.

Depression can also bring with it a spiritual paralysis. It's difficult to concentrate, so any sort of reading can be a problem. Our mind is in

Mark 2:1–5

turmoil thanks to the ever-present unfocused anxiety tying our thinking processes into knots. Praying can, for many reasons, be beyond our capabilities, and in any case our faith itself may be frozen and unable to bring us to God.

So even if Jesus was in a house nearby and he was healing people I'm not sure that, in the depths of depression, I would be able to get there or would want to. It would involve too much pain and trauma of mind, body and spirit to be possible. But I might agree to friends taking me to Jesus.

We need people who will do for us what we cannot or won't do for ourselves. We need the grace to allow our friends to help and support us and to bring us in prayer to God without us having to take any sort of initiative.

After some days he returned to Capernaum, and news went round that he was at home; and such a crowd collected that there was no room for them even in the space outside the door. While he was proclaiming the message to them, a man was brought who was paralysed. Four men were carrying him, but because of the crowd they could not get him near. So they made an opening in the roof over the place where Jesus was, and when they had broken through they lowered the bed on which the paralysed man was lying. When he saw their faith, Jesus said to the man, "My son, your sins are forgiven."

Mark 2:1-5

When he saw their faith,
Jesus said to the man, "My
son, your sins are forgiven."

Feelings of guilt and shame are familiar to many of us who go through depression. The feelings may well be unfocused and be as much about who we are as about what we've done. Our distorted thinking and perception of ourselves can convince us that somehow we "deserve" this "punishment" and that we don't "deserve" to get better.

These powerful and negative beliefs about ourselves only add to the paralysis of the mind and spirit we've just been thinking about. If we believe that somehow we deserve this suffering, why would we look for the strength and will to challenge these thought processes?

If this is how depression affects us, it might be quite hard to hear Jesus saying, "your sins are forgiven", since it might suggest that the illness is indeed a punishment, thus confirming the distortions in our thinking.

On the other hand, the words "your sins are forgiven" might bring hope and the promise of new life into our hearts where our deepest hurts lie.

When depression makes life seem out of control

So they came to the country of the Gerasenes on the other side of the lake. As he stepped ashore, a man possessed by an unclean spirit came up to him from among the tombs where he had made his home. Nobody could control him any longer; even chains were useless, for he had often been fettered and chained up, but had snapped his chains and broken the fetters. No one was strong enough to master him.

Unceasingly, night and day, he would cry aloud among the tombs and on the hillsides and gash himself with stones.

5:2-5

Our next encounter is with a tormented man, a man who is an outcast and "unclean" for many reasons.

We might think we have little in common with this poor man, but let's look again at Mark's description of him and what happens when he encounters Jesus.

The man is beyond the control of himself and others. Nobody can calm him down and talk with him rationally. There is a barrier of fear separating the possessed from "normal" people.

At some point this man has been chained up and fettered, presumably to prevent him harming others.

Today if a person is mentally ill and is perceived to be a danger to himself or herself and/or to others he or she can also be "fettered" by being "sectioned" or "detained" (in Britain, this would be under the Mental Health Act 1983). It may be that in our society that is the best way we know of caring for those whose minds are so disturbed or damaged while also protecting others. But it can also, I think, reinforce ideas about punishment, fear and isolation.

The appalling nature of this man's illness leads him to cry out his torment twenty-four hours a day and to gash himself with stones – a very early example of self-harming. We may not know why we do it. Perhaps physical pain distracts our mind from the internal pain; perhaps it's a form of self-punishment inflicted because we believe we are such bad and awful people.

If our mental distress causes:

- *lack of control over our emotions;*
- *chaotic or unhealthy lifestyles;*
- *others to fear us;*
- *isolation from society; or*
- *self-harming*

then I think we can identify in some way with this man who now rushes to Jesus.

The phrase "to be possessed" suggests that a person is no longer free to make choices about who he or she wants to be or what to do at any given time. It suggests that something more powerful has taken control and is driving us.

My experience of depression is that it can be described in similar ways. If we are physically ill or injured, our sickness is visible and understood. Perhaps more importantly, we remain ourselves – possibly less patient or active, but basically our personality remains intact. When depression descends, though, our personality can change, our thought processes are disrupted, our memory is affected, our view of people, relationships and life in general is distorted and we can no longer lead our everyday lives. It goes to the heart of who we are as a person.

So in that sense we can experience depression as something that takes over and possesses our lives so we are no longer free to be our true selves.

Our true identity is being eaten up by this invisible monster and we no longer have the mental or emotional resources to resist.

If we experience depression in this way, perhaps we need to deal with it in a way that honours that experience. A friend of mine who had cancer told me once that she was encouraged to visualise the illness and it being attacked by the chemicals she was receiving in her treatment. Perhaps we too can be encouraged to visualise our depression as a usurper, an enemy within. Churchill called his depression the "black dog". I have an unprintable name for mine! Maybe we need to use the language of demon possession to make some sense of what's happening.

When he saw Jesus in the distance, he ran up and flung himself down before him, shouting at the top of his voice, "What do you want with me, Jesus, Son of the Most High God? In God's name do not torment me." For Jesus was already saying to him, "Out, unclean spirit, come out of the man!" Jesus asked him, "What is your name?" "My name is Legion," he said, "there are so many of us."

Mark 5:6-9

If we follow the next part of the story visualising our depressive demons as the demons ordered out by Jesus, it might give us a very powerful picture of God fighting on our side to free us from our wretchedness. Look what happens:

> *There was a large herd of pigs nearby, feeding on the hillside, and the spirits begged Jesus, "Send us among the pigs; let us go into them." He gave them leave; and the unclean spirits came out and went into the pigs; and the herd, of about two thousand, rushed over the edge into the lake and were drowned.*

That's a picture to hold on to!

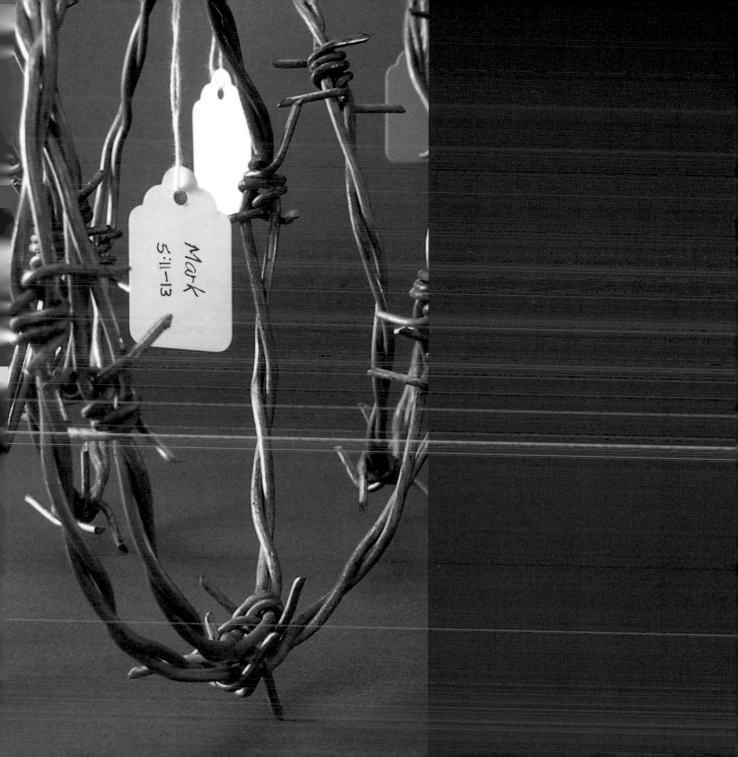

Mark
5:11–13

Adjusting to a new life

The man who was possessed by so many demons that his name was "Legion" has been freed from their clutches. It looks like a happy ending, but then this happens:

> *The men in charge of [the pigs] took to their heels and carried the news to the town and countryside; and the people came out to see what had happened. When they came to Jesus and saw the madman who had been possessed by the legion of demons, sitting there clothed and in his right mind, they were afraid. When eyewitnesses told them what had happened to the madman and what had become of the pigs, they begged Jesus to leave the district.*

The encounter with Jesus has changed the man beyond recognition; and what a wonderful contrast to see him now seated next to Jesus, clothed, calm and in his right mind. He has regained his identity. The fragmented pieces of his self have been restored to their right places. He is not Legion any more. He is one man, no longer a danger to himself or others, but still somewhat apart from his community, who are afraid. They're afraid because:

- *he seems well now, but will it last?*
- *we can talk to him now, but will he always have his reason?*
- *he's safe now, but how far dare we trust him?*
- *will he continue to take his medication?*

Interestingly, they send Jesus away. Perhaps they hope this man will go with him and not be their problem if he does have a relapse. The man himself would prefer to go with Jesus:

As he was getting into the boat, the man who had been possessed begged to go with him. But Jesus would not let him. "Go home to your own people," he said, "and tell them what the Lord in his mercy has done for you."
Mark 5:18-19

I've always found this ending of the story very poignant and it often stirs up in me a feeling of deep sadness, loneliness and vulnerability. I see it through my own experience of separations and losses over the years, some of them caused by this illness. I see this nameless man as alone and lonely, not understood, afraid and without hope. Then along comes a stranger who isn't afraid, who is compassionate and powerful, and who understands the problem and what's needed. Through this stranger he is freed, made well and given a chance to begin again.

Then the stranger has to leave. Perhaps the man too has his own fears:

- *what will happen if I'm ill again?*
- *perhaps I'm only well while he's here.*
- *how will I cope?*
- *who else can understand what it's like?*

However he feels, though, he is given the strength to remain and do as Jesus asks him, and two thousand years later he is still telling us what the Lord in his mercy did for him.

His story tells us that Jesus has the power to set us free from everything that is harming our minds, distorting our thinking, threatening our identity and keeping us from him.

If it hasn't already come, there will be a time when we too are sent out to tell our own stories about what the Lord in his mercy has done for us.

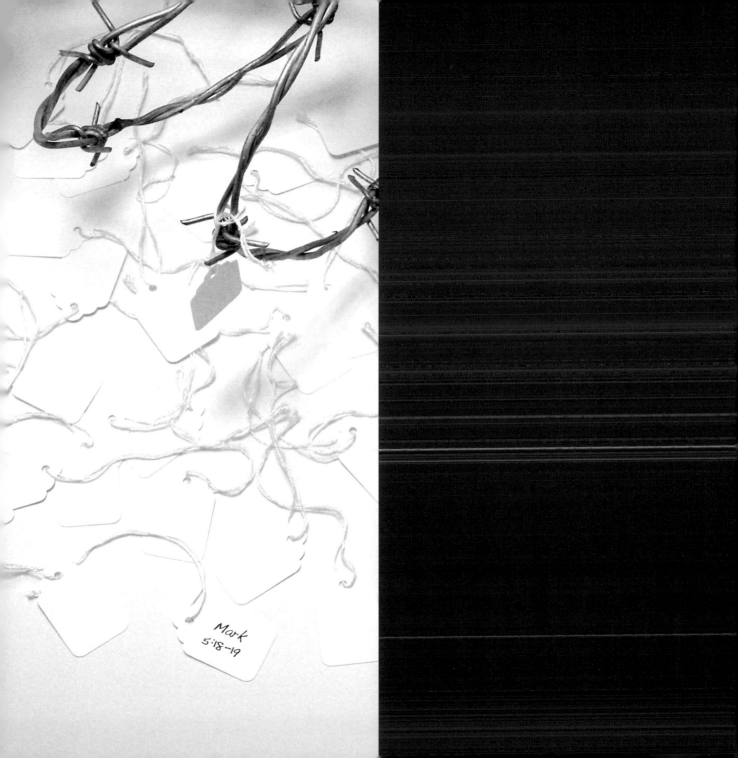

Mark
5:18-19

Illness is embarrassing

We now meet another person whose predicament has elements with which we can empathise. Again, her encounter with Jesus may help us to gain new insight into our own search for healing and acceptance.

Among [the crowd] was a woman who had suffered from haemorrhages for twelve years; and in spite of long treatment by many doctors, on which she had spent all she had, she had become worse rather than better.

Mark 5:25–26

This woman's illness has hurt her in many ways. The loss of blood over so many years must surely have taken its toll on her energy levels. I imagine she must have been drained and exhausted most of the time and perhaps vulnerable to all sorts of other ailments as her body's defences have been weakened. On top of these debilitating symptoms she has had to spend money on consulting doctors and paying for their various remedies. If she herself doesn't have money, and that would seem very likely in that society, she is dependent on some male relative for any treatment she has. But still, after twelve years, she has not made any recovery. In fact, we are told, things have got worse.

While this woman is bleeding she is considered "unclean", which must have had a devastating effect on her. It has isolated her and prevented her having a normal, healthy, sexual relationship with a man. It may have prevented her getting married or having children. If so, in a culture where a woman is shamed if she doesn't bear a child, she will have been stigmatised and will probably remain alone and shunned.

So in a very few words Mark gives us an idea of the situation this woman is in, how humiliating it is for her and how desperate she must be for healing and freedom from her sickness.

Depression, too, can be a very long-term illness. It can lurk in the background, sometimes unnoticed, before flaring up and demanding attention. We may have known its presence in our lives for many years; we may even not know life without it. We've already seen that depression is debilitating and we can get into a downward spiral of decreasing energy, exhaustion and weakness so that our general condition gets worse rather than better.

Depression is also persistent and stubborn and sometimes, unfortunately, it takes a long time to find a way through so that at least we become able to "manage" it and lead lives free of its all-encompassing presence.

We are able to see our GPs without charge in Britain, but unfortunately resources available to mental health services through the NHS are limited and under intense pressure. In many other countries, everything has to be paid for. There are many effective medicines for treating depression but they usually take a number of weeks to begin working, and it may also take a while to find the most suitable drug for each individual – there is no "one size fits all". There are usually waiting lists for any kind of "talking therapy" – a wait during which things may well deteriorate even further.

Many of us look to "complementary" or "alternative" medicine as either a main or an additional treatment. Some find them effective while others don't, and again we may need to try various options. Consultations and remedies in this "private" sphere are expensive and often outside our budget. If we add the cost of private counselling or psychotherapy we can see how quickly this course of treatment may cause us to spend all we have with no guarantee of success.

We might well find ourselves, like this woman, at the end of our tether, desperate for healing, powerless to seek more professional help and needing a miracle.

She had heard about Jesus, and came up behind him in the crowd and touched his cloak; for she said, "If I touch even his clothes, I shall be healed."

And there and then the flow of blood dried up and she knew in herself that she was cured of her affliction.

Mark 5:27-29

The woman knows that Jesus can heal people with all sorts of ailments. She's probably seen the way he touches those in need and watched the changes take place within them or on their limbs, skin or face. Why does she not go to him openly and ask him for help? She may be ashamed of her illness, embarrassed to draw attention to it in front of a crowd of people, many of them men. She knows, too, that if Jesus does touch her, he will himself become unclean, and perhaps she fears being blamed and sent away without a cure.

Whatever her reason for not openly approaching Jesus, we can probably identify with her. Depression, too, can be something we feel ashamed of and embarrassed to talk about; or we fear rejection and dismissal from someone who cannot understand us. I once sought help from a GP who, after five minutes, dismissed me because, he said, he had to see patients "who really are ill".

So if we believe, like this woman, that Jesus has the power to heal, we might prefer to seek his healing secretly, alone, hoping that if we just make contact, somehow we will be healed.

Aware at once that power had gone out of him, Jesus turned round in the crowd and asked, "Who touched my clothes?" His disciples said to him, "You see the crowd pressing round you and yet you ask, 'Who touched me?'" But he kept looking around to see who had done it.

Mark 5:30-32

I wonder how the woman feels as she tries to slip away without being noticed: greatly relieved, perhaps, and excited that now she is healed and "clean"? A bit guilty about "taking" healing rather than asking for it? A bit ashamed at bringing her uncleanness into a crowd?

Whatever she feels, she doesn't expect Jesus to be aware of what she's done, and his question startles her. She seems to know immediately that Jesus is looking for her.

As we've seen earlier, for Jesus, someone in great need, someone who seeks him out but is too afraid or too ashamed to approach him openly, is a person he needs to find and heal. He cannot give up the search when he knows he's needed by a lost, lonely and distressed child of God. Jesus knows the depth of our needs and is doing all he can to bring about change and growth into wholeness.

Then the woman, trembling with fear because she knew what had happened to her, came and fell at his feet and told him the whole truth. He said to her, "Daughter, your faith has healed you. Go in peace, free from your affliction."

The ending of this story, for me, is deeply moving.

The woman is frightened. Jesus seems to be very keen to see who it was who touched him. Perhaps she fears the healing will be annulled because she "took" it from him.

With amazing courage, though, she comes forward to him and tells him what she's done and why, and how she knows she has been healed.

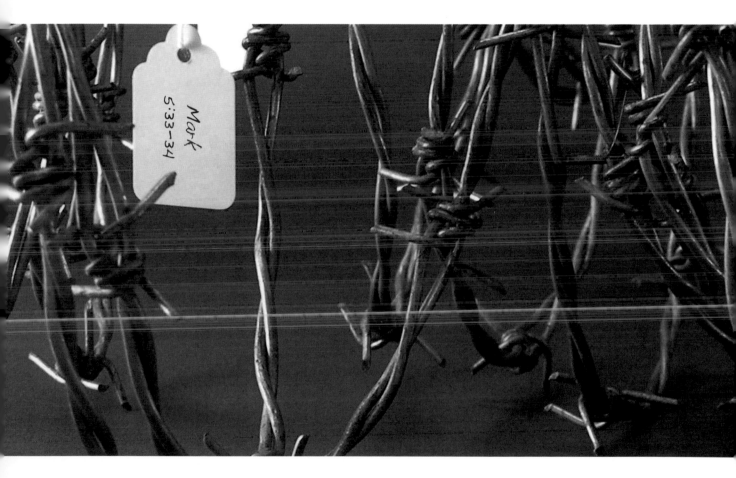

I think it would still be a courageous thing for a woman today to talk openly to a man, in front of a lot of strangers (no doubt many looking very disapprovingly at her), about intimate gynaecological problems.

It takes courage to trust someone enough to talk openly about how we feel, or it takes sheer desperation, when we believe we are just not being heard or taken seriously. But when we do have the courage to be totally honest before God and tell him the whole truth, that truth does set us free in ways that might seem impossible to us now.

And the reaction of Jesus is to affirm her faith with loving words which send her on her way "in peace, free from [her] affliction".

There are a couple of points coming out of this story which I'd like to explore a little further.

Over the years my experience has been that growth and change only take place when I can be very honest, at least in my own mind, about how I feel, what I want and where I know I'm not allowing change to happen.

I've always kept a journal, and often it's only in there that I've been able to express honestly my thoughts, words and deeds with all their shortcomings, failures and lack of love.

The act of writing so openly and honestly, painful though it can be, has often proved to be a turning point, offering an opportunity for God's healing and forgiveness to reach me.

The fact that I know that, unless I choose otherwise, this writing will never be shared with anyone gives me a freedom to be honest and to write something that I can then offer

to God as prayer. For me, writing in my journal is praying and when I read back over past entries I can often see how God has answered my prayers (sometimes in ways I didn't recognise at the time), and so my faith in answered prayer is confirmed and strengthened.

Being totally honest with another person, though, is a different matter. I think we are right and wise to be extremely careful about whom we trust and confide in. If confidences are betrayed or if we're met with an unsympathetic or critical response, we can't turn the clock back and stay silent.

I've made errors of judgement about a person's discretion or ability to understand the experience of depression and got badly hurt. But I've also had, and still have, the love, friendship and support of some pretty amazing people, and I'm very grateful for that.

I think we each have to make our own decisions about whom we trust, and it isn't easy at a time when our ability to make such judgements and decisions is under pressure and strain. Perhaps the best thing we can do is pray for God's guidance about trusting people and take it very gently for our own protection.

When my self-esteem was at its lowest ebb and my disgust with myself was at its worst, I could buy some clothes that looked good in the shop but once they became mine I saw them as dirty, revolting, contaminated somehow simply by being connected to me.

I had similar experiences about all sorts of things and people, believing that I was "unclean" and ought to warn others to keep away from me in case they too were contaminated. I thought that others must see that that's what I was like and so felt ashamed and bad for having the gall to behave as if I was "clean".

These experiences may be familiar to other sufferers and it's important to remember that this is part of the illness – it's a false reality, no matter how convincing it seems to be. When we are aware of people not being able to cope with our illness, avoiding us or judging us, our belief in ourselves as somehow tainted is only confirmed.

The story of the woman who had been bleeding for twelve years alerts me to a great truth about Jesus and about God. We cannot make him unclean by our lack of cleanliness. It's his healing energy and power that flow out to us, not our "sin" that contaminates him.

Jesus is not afraid of "catching" our illness. He is not threatened by it or revolted. Instead he is the one who looks for us and calls us forward to receive his gift and blessing.

he is the one who looks for us

Struggling to believe

A man in the crowd spoke up: "Teacher, I brought my son for you to cure. He is possessed by a spirit that makes him dumb. Whenever it attacks him, it flings him to the ground, and he foams at the mouth, grinds his teeth and goes rigid"... Jesus answered "Bring him to me." So they brought the boy to him; and as soon as the spirit saw him it threw the boy into convulsions, and he fell on the ground and rolled about foaming at the mouth. Jesus asked his father, "How long has he been like this?" "From childhood," he replied.

Mark 9:17-18, 19-21

The father describes his son as being possessed by a spirit, although the symptoms described also sound like epilepsy.

In a sense it doesn't really matter what is causing the convulsions. What is important for us here are the words and behaviour of the three main characters in the story: Jesus, the father and the son.

As we've already seen, depression can be present for a long time before being properly diagnosed and treated. Children can suffer from it, and it may be that some of us can't remember a time when this great dark cloud didn't hang over us.

If this is the case, then it may also be true that it's hard for us to imagine what life would be like without the cloud. We're not sure what that would feel like and how it might affect our sense of self and our relationships with other people.

We might well have a sense of dying and being born again into a new life, and then learning how to be our new selves in our new surroundings.

Of course it also means that our families, friends and colleagues will find that their perception of us also has to change and grow. That could well be difficult for them, and it's possible that some relationships cannot be that flexible. But the good news is that family bonds and friendships can become deeper, more "real" and more trusting than before. As we recover and heal, so too broken and strained relationships can be mended and strengthened by the God of reconciliation and peace.

The father continues to speak, giving Jesus, and us, a picture of how his son's life is frequently in danger both from the convulsions themselves and from the way in which the convulsions put the son in harm's way:

> *"From childhood," [the father] replied. "It has often tried to destroy him by throwing him into the fire or into water."*

It must have been incredibly painful and frightening for this father to watch his son having these convulsions, knowing that one day they might cause his death.

When someone you love is suffering from depression, it's painful to see the effects of the illness, the way it changes its victims and distorts their outlook on life.

Sufferers can also be led into danger in a variety of ways:

- *The need for love and comfort can lead to unhealthy and perhaps suffocating closeness to someone in sometimes most inappropriate contexts.*
- *Guilt and shame, self-hatred and pent-up anger can lead to distressing self-harming/punishing.*
- *Unchecked anxiety, panic or despair can lead to suicidal feelings, or at least a need to escape consciousness, which can in turn lead on to an overdose of medication or some other form of self-destructive behaviour.*

If you yourself are in this sort of situation, or if someone you know is in this sort of danger, I would urge you, if it's not already in place, to seek some kind of specialist therapeutic intervention.

These issues of unhealthy and sometimes dangerous relationships and the physical expression of self-hatred and self-destructiveness are, I believe, likely to have very deep and early roots.

Like the earth and the dirt that, over centuries, became caked on to my vase, so too can layers of experiences, emotions and memories (conscious or unconscious) build up around us, hiding our true selves from the world.

Like the vase, we too need careful treatment from specialists who understand our vulnerabilities and fragility as bit by bit we work through all the layers of mud. This can be a very long, slow process and unfortunately there aren't many short cuts but, like the vase, we too are infinitely precious and beautiful to God, and he will protect and hold us close while we're in danger.

As I read the story of this man and his son, and how the son's illness has troubled them both for so long, I feel sure that the father is in need of healing as much as the son is. He has had to watch his son go through these dreadful convulsions and protect him from any dangers around at the time. He's never known when the next attack will be, or where, and he must be very anxious for his son's future. So when the father says, "take pity on us and help us", I can imagine Jesus reaching out to him to set his mind at rest as well and I'm sure that in the same way Jesus reaches out to those who love and care for a sufferer of mental distress and pain.

In my experience, carers, family and friends can often get overlooked when someone is mentally ill and needing treatment. It can be very distressing for them and they may feel inadequate in the face of deeply ingrained ways of thinking and feeling, found in themselves, in the sufferer and in those they meet, and which are causing such deep distress to someone they love, and preventing healing, change and growth taking place.

It is important that the people most affected by someone's illness find some sort of respite from the relentless draining of energy, the constant stress of not knowing what to expect next and the weight of hopelessness that threatens to pull down everyone within its reach.

If family, friends and carers can find some sort of support and respite, I think that in itself can break a cycle of everyone involved worrying about everyone else – it allows some fresh air to start moving within the relationships, easing some of the tensions and charging up people's batteries for the continuing climb out of the pit.

And in all of this we might forget that God is with us, loving each one and holding us in his heart.

> *Fear not, for I have redeemed you.*
> *I have called you by name, you are mine.*
> *When you pass through the waters, I will be with you.*
> *When you walk through fire, you shall not be burned.*
> Isaiah 43:1-2

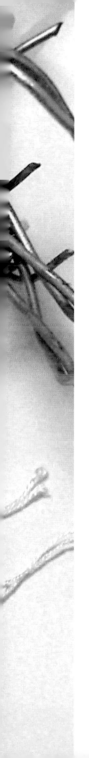

In this story the father says to Jesus:

But if it is at all possible for you, take pity on us and help us.

And Jesus replies:

If it is possible! Everything is possible to one who believes.

This assurance is for us today in the same way it was for our ancestors in faith. It's an assurance to hang on to when everything looks totally overwhelming and we feel we're at the absolute limit of what we can cope with.

But then there's that little proviso at the end of Jesus' response: "… to one who believes".

And the father speaks for all of us who struggle to believe against the odds and for all of us who daren't believe wholeheartedly for fear of disappointment or rejection.

I believe; help my unbelief.

For a long time now this cry of faith and longing has been for me a liberating and almost joyful prayer.

I believe as far as I'm able to believe in anything. I believe you are there and that for you all things are possible. I offer to you the faith I do have and ask you to help me to have more.

And then I realise that this prayer need not be just about faith, and immediately other prayers are formed in my mind:

> *I love; help my unloving.*
> *I hope; help my unhoping.*
> *I give; help my ungiving.*
> *I care; help my uncaring.*
> *I want to be well; help my unwanting.*

And I realise that I can offer to God all that's good and healthy in me already, no matter how little that seems to me. God will look after the goodness for me; he won't let me lose the little I have. Instead he will work with me to put right the parts that are not so good and healthy until I am transformed into his likeness.

It seems as though Jesus would have continued talking with the father but:

> *When Jesus saw that the crowd was closing in on them, he spoke directly to the unclean spirit. "Deaf and dumb spirit," he said, "I command you come out of him and never go back!" It shrieked aloud and threw the boy into repeated convulsions, and then came out, leaving him looking like a corpse; in fact, many said, "He is dead." But Jesus took hold of his hand and raised him to his feet, and he stood up.*
>
> Mark 9:25-27

The father had enough faith, it seems. Jesus takes the faith that is offered and the son is released – but at a cost. The boy has first to endure a violent onslaught of the convulsions, which leaves him totally wiped out – so much so that some think he has finally been killed by his affliction.

Sadly it is true that sometimes bad things have to get worse before they get better. We've seen before how painful healing and recovery can be, and maybe sometimes we almost wish we could go back to where we were before.

It's like the stage we get to when redecorating a room: we've stripped wallpaper and plaster has fallen off the ceiling, we've sanded the woodwork and taken out an old fire, and it all looks horrible and messy, disrupting our lives and somehow making the rest of the house look almost as bad. We can't go back – we're well beyond the point of no return – we just need to remind ourselves of what the refurbished room is going to look like, and keep working!

While struggling through our own refurbishment, let's remember and hold on to this image:

Jesus took hold of his hand and raised him to his feet, and he stood up.

Jesus takes us by the hand and raises us to our feet, and one day we too will stand up and walk away from whatever has held us captive.

Part Three

The Day *of* Resurrection

It's hard when you're enduring Good Friday to imagine the dawning of Easter Day.

Susan Howatch
A Question of Integrity

We're coming towards the end of our journey together. We've been through some difficult times and may not be ready yet for Easter Day to dawn in our lives.

Recovery is not a steady, smooth progression and we often find ourselves travelling along old familiar paths. Experience tells me, though, that when we revisit a dark place we often do so on a different level which brings new insights and a different perspective. Our illness may not be completely over, but we will change our relationship with it and learn to live more freely.

A thought that I still hang on to is that it was only from the tomb that Jesus could rise to new life; it is only from the darkness of night that a new day can dawn; it is in the wilderness that God does a new thing in our lives and his angels minister to us even, or especially, when we feel most alone and isolated.

The prayer of all who care for you is that you will be brought safely through the wilderness and that you will walk, wounded but also renewed, into the sunrise of Easter Day.

When the Sabbath was over, Mary of Magdala, Mary the mother of James, and Salome bought aromatic oils, intending to go and anoint him; and very early on the first day of the week, just after sunrise, they came to the tomb.

They went into the tomb, where they saw a young man sitting on the right-hand side, wearing a white robe; and they were dumbfounded. But he said to them, "Do not be alarmed; you are looking for Jesus of Nazareth, who was crucified. He has been raised; he is not here. Look there is the place where they laid him. But go and say to his disciples and to Peter: 'He is going ahead of you into Galilee: there you will see him, as he told you.' " Then they went out and ran away from the tomb, trembling with amazement. They said nothing to anyone, for they were afraid.

Mark 16:1 8

It's the perfect Easter morning: the sun is shining and there's not even a wisp of a cloud in the sky. The air is clear with the lightest of breezes to remind us that it's not summertime yet. The daffodils are out, the cherry blossom is unfolding: "Jesus Christ is risen today. Alleluia!"

Evidence of new life is all around us and there's good news of hope and promise, redemption and resurrection.

Who could help but be uplifted, encouraged, joyful and filled with new energy and commitment?

I think that if you're a stranger to depression it must be very hard to understand the potential impact of this illness on your whole being, at all times.

In the past I've found that being in church on Easter Sunday can be an extremely lonely and painful experience. I wonder sometimes if it's better not to go, but then I have a glimmer of hope that perhaps this year I will experience light in my darkness and resurrection into a new way of being.

I don't think it's surprising that sometimes we can feel this devastation on Easter Day, not when we set it in the context of the weeks leading up to it.

Ever since Ash Wednesday our internal state of depression and some of its manifestations have been in keeping with, or "in tune" with, the liturgy in our services and the general "flavour" of the season of Lent. For example:

- *The call for close self-examination and the emphasis on our need for repentance and forgiveness is in tune with our deep introspection, self-hatred and guilt. We overlook the fact that these are symptoms of an illness and that they do not reflect the reality of who we are.*

- *We need to find a balance between our unhealthy and destructive perception of ourselves and a healthy regret for the shortcomings and weaknesses that are part of everyday life for everyone.*

- *The tradition of self-discipline, prayer and study of scripture is in tune with our relentless driving of ourselves to do better, to be perfect and to attain God's approval. What should be nourishing and life-giving becomes a duty, a pressure, another thing to fail at, another reason to punish ourselves.*

- *This is one of those heavy burdens we place upon ourselves. I believe that actually God would much prefer us to rest, to go easy on ourselves and allow him some time and space to minister to us in whatever way he can.*

- *As we move into Passiontide, Holy Week, Maundy Thursday and Good Friday, the ever-darkening clouds descend and, more than ever, our liturgies and readings resonate with our own personal Good Friday experience. Perhaps we feel in closer fellowship with other people in church as together we follow the way that leads to the cross.*

- *Then suddenly, overnight, the mood around us changes as Easter Day dawns and we are left behind, once again alone in Gethsemane or at Golgotha, praying for deliverance and feeling utterly forsaken.*

For all of us who have suffered loss, or despair, Easter can be a very painful time when a hollow emptiness within us can't be filled by singing hymns of joy and seeing flowers decorate the cross of suffering.

If our Good Friday experience has to be endured over many, many days and at any time in the year, so too can Easter Day dawn unexpectedly in our hearts at any time.

- *There are two mornings in one week when we wake up and that wave of hopelessness and dread doesn't immediately wash over us.*

- *There's a day when we can do some household chore without being wiped out for the next few hours.*

- *There's a time when we decide we want to walk down to a local shop rather than stay inside because we can't face meeting anyone.*

- *There's some music on the radio that touches our heart with its beauty and is no longer background noise to keep silence at bay.*

- *We read a book and are actually interested in the characters and storyline.*

Easter Day dawns in many different ways, blossom gradually unfolds and fresh air begins to flow into previously closed-in places of our lives.

It's entirely understandable if, like the two Marys and Salome at the empty tomb, we tremble with amazement and say nothing to anyone because we're afraid.

We're afraid because we've known many false dawns when a new hope has sunk back down towards despair, when a burst of energy has resulted in an exhaustion deeper than ever, when enjoyable music or a good book has changed back into a meaningless distraction. The trouble with these apparently false dawns is that the outlook seems even worse because we believed they might be true and we punish ourselves for

being so stupid, vowing never to be deceived again.

But what if these dawns aren't so false after all? What if we dare to begin to believe in them as signs of life from that tiny seed of hope that was sown long ago: "I am and will be healed"? What if we treat these moments very gently, allowing them just to be, without poking at them to see if they're real or trying to force their growth by our own efforts? Let's just very quietly acknowledge and believe in these tiny signs of hope and life.

At last, there's a week when we wake up more times free of dread than not. At last we stay awake and active for whole days at a time and so start sleeping better at night. At last we actually want to meet with friends and at last we begin to believe that life is regaining colour, scent, taste, and, above all, hope and purpose.

Just as depression feeds on itself and creates its own downward spiral into the pit, so too healing and hope build on themselves, creating new paths for us to travel.

Two weeks of relief from the overwhelming darkness lead us to believe the next two might also bring light back into our world. A month of being able to go for walks leads us to better physical health with the energy to go further. Three evenings spent with friends lead us to believe we can be with other people without withdrawing into ourselves and needing to get away.

Each time we take two steps forward, the almost inevitable one step back becomes less frightening as we learn that it doesn't mean we're going to go all the way down to the depths of the pit.

Our recovery may seem slow, but we don't always realise how ill we've been and how far we've come. However, when we look back over a period of six weeks/three months/a year we'll see that although there have been ups and downs, good days and bad days, overall we've been making sure and steady progress, and there's no reason to think that progress won't continue.

The two Marys and Salome must have told someone something eventually when they overcame their fear. One day we too will speak of the dawning of Easter Day and the resurrection that God has brought about in our lives. We will speak and say that Christ has risen, he has risen indeed.

Alleluia!

I love the Lord,
for he has heard the voice of my
supplication;
because he inclined his ear to me
on the day I called to him.

The snares of death encompassed
me;
the pains of hell took hold of me;
by grief and sorrow was I held.

Then I called upon the name of the
Lord;
"O Lord, I beg you, deliver my
soul."

Gracious is the Lord and righteous;
our God is full of compassion.

The Lord watches over the simple;
I was brought very low and he
saved me.

Turn again to your rest, O my soul,
for the Lord has been gracious to
you.

For you have delivered my soul
from death, my eyes from tears
and my feet from falling.

I will walk before the Lord
in the land of the living.
I believed that I should perish
for I was sorely troubled;
and I said in my alarm,
"Everyone is a liar."

How shall I repay the Lord
for all the benefits he has given to
me?

I will lift up the cup of salvation
and call upon the name of the
Lord.

I will fulfil my vows to the Lord
in the presence of all his people.

Precious in the sight of the Lord
is the death of his faithful servants.

O Lord, I am your servant,
your servant, the child of your
handmaid; you have freed me from
my bonds.

I will offer to you a sacrifice of
thanksgiving and call upon the
name of the Lord.

I will fulfil my vows to the Lord
in the presence of all his people.

In the courts of the house of
the Lord, in the midst of you, O
Jerusalem.

Alleluia.

Psalm 116
(*Common Worship* Psalter)